WHO'S WHO OF PRO SPORTS

WHO'S WHO OF

A GUIDE TO THE GAME'S GREATEST PLAYERS

by Shane Frederick

CAPSTONE PRESS
a capstone imprint

Sports Illustrated Kids Who's Who of Pro Sports are published by Capstone Press,
1710 Roe Crest Drive, North Mankato, Minnesota 56003
www.capstonepub.com

Library of Congress Cataloging-in-Publication Data
Frederick, Shane.
  Who's who of pro hockey : a guide to the game's greatest players / by Shane Frederick.
      pages cm.—(Sports illustrated kids. Who's who of pro sports)
  Includes bibliographical references and index.
  Summary: "Introduces readers to the most dynamic pro hockey stars of today and yesterday, including
notable statistics and records"—Provided by publisher.
  ISBN 978-1-4765-5797-7 (library binding)
  ISBN 978-1-4914-7609-3 (eBook PDF)
1. Hockey players—Biography—Juvenile literature. 2. Hockey players—Rating of—Juvenile literature.
I. Title.

  GV848.5.A1F746 2016
  796.9620922—dc23
  [B]
                          2015002811

Editorial Credits
Nate LeBoutillier, editor; Kyle Grenz, designer; Eric Gohl, media researcher

Photo Credits
Getty Images: Melchior DiGiacomo, 23 (top); Newscom: Icon SMI/IHA, 19, ZUMA Press/Dick Darrell,
22; Shutterstock: Isantilli, 6; Sports Illustrated: Bob Rosato, 14, Damian Strohmeyer, 26, David E. Klutho,
cover (middle), 4, 5, 8, 9, 10 (all), 11, 15, 16, 17, 20, 21, 23 (bottom), 27, 28, John D. Hanlon, 13, John G.
Zimmerman, cover (right), 25, John Iacono, 24, Manny Millan, 18, Robert Beck, 12, Simon Bruty, 7, Tony
Triolo, cover (left)

Design Elements: Shutterstock

Printed in the United States of America in North Mankato, Minnesota.
042015   008823CGF15

TABLE OF CONTENTS

RULERS OF THE RINK

For nearly a century, the National Hockey League (NHL) has thrilled fans throughout North America. Players skate at blazing speeds, launch rocket shots, and deliver bone-crushing checks. They make precision passes, sneaky steals, acrobatic saves, and brave blocks. At the end of a long, tough season, the best teams then play for one of sports' most-prized trophies, the Stanley Cup. But who are these players who have made hockey such an exciting sport? Which teams have battled to be the best time and time again? It's time to find out Who's Who in the NHL.

WAYNE **GRETZKY**

5

Chapter 1

LATEST GREATS

They Have Hart

After each NHL season, the Hart Trophy is given to the most valuable player (MVP) in the league. Check out this list of Hart Trophy winners from the past 15 NHL seasons.

REMARKABLE RECORDS

Joe Thornton is the only MVP to play for two teams in the same season. In 2005–06, the Boston Bruins traded him to the San Jose Sharks.

Year:	Most Valuable Player:
2000	Chris **Pronger**, D, St. Louis Blues
2001	Joe **Sakic**, C, Colorado Avalanche
2002	Jose **Theodore**, G, Montreal Canadiens
2003	Peter **Forsberg**, C, Colorado Avalanche
2004	Martin **St. Louis**, RW, Tampa Bay Lightning
2005	NHL season canceled due to lockout
2006	Joe **Thornton**, C, San Jose Sharks
2007	Sidney **Crosby**, C, Pittsburgh Penguins
2008	Alex **Ovechkin**, LW, Washington Capitals
2009	Alex **Ovechkin**, LW, Washington Capitals
2010	Henrik **Sedin**, C, Vancouver Canucks
2011	Corey **Perry**, RW, Anaheim Ducks
2012	Evgeni **Malkin**, C, Pittsburgh Penguins
2013	Alex **Ovechkin**, RW, Washington Capitals
2014	Sidney **Crosby**, C, Pittsburgh Penguins

Back-to-Back

Sporting a gap-toothed grin and signature yellow laces on his skates, Alex Ovechkin isn't hard to miss. Unless you're an opposing player charged with slowing him down, that is. Since joining the NHL in 2005, the bull-rushing Washington Capitals winger from Russia has been one of the sport's most feared scorers. In 2009 he became the first player to win back-to-back Hart Trophies since goalie Dominik Hasek collected his second in 1998. When he won again in 2013, Ovechkin became he first to claim three MVPs since the great Mario Lemieux earned his third in 1993.

ALEX OVECHKIN

STAT-TASTIC

In 2006–07, 19-year-old Sidney Crosby scored 120 points. He became the youngest scoring champion ever in a North American team sport.

Whose Line Starts?

Hockey is a game played in shifts, with forward lines and defensive pairings taking turns skating as the game goes on. Imagine what the line chart of an NHL Dream Team of recent star players might look like:

Left Wing	Center	Right Wing
Joe **Pavelski**, Sharks	Sidney **Crosby**, Penguins	Alex **Ovechkin**, Capitals
Daniel **Sedin**, Canucks	Henrik **Sedin**, Canucks	Corey **Perry**, Ducks
Jamie **Benn**, Stars	Jonathan **Toews**, Blackhawks	Phil **Kessel**, Maple Leafs
Zach **Parise**, Wild	Steven **Stamkos**, Lightning	Patrick **Kane**, Blackhawks

Defenseman	Goaltender	Defenseman
Duncan **Keith**, Blackhawks	Henrik **Lundqvist**, Rangers	P.K. **Subban**, Canadiens
Shea **Weber**, Predators	Jonathan **Quick**, Kings	Erik **Karlsson**, Senators
Zdeno **Chara**, Bruins	Tuukka **Rask**, Bruins	Drew **Doughty**, Kings

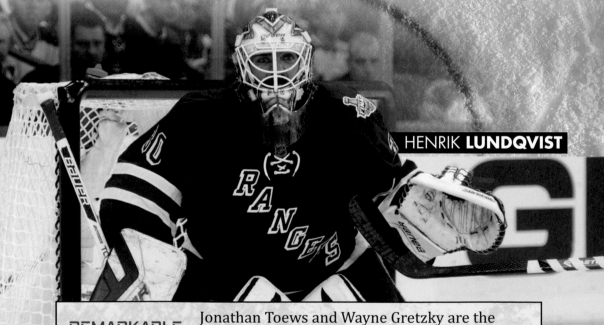

HENRIK **LUNDQVIST**

REMARKABLE RECORDS Jonathan Toews and Wayne Gretzky are the only players in NHL history to captain two Stanley Cup-winning teams before the age of 25.

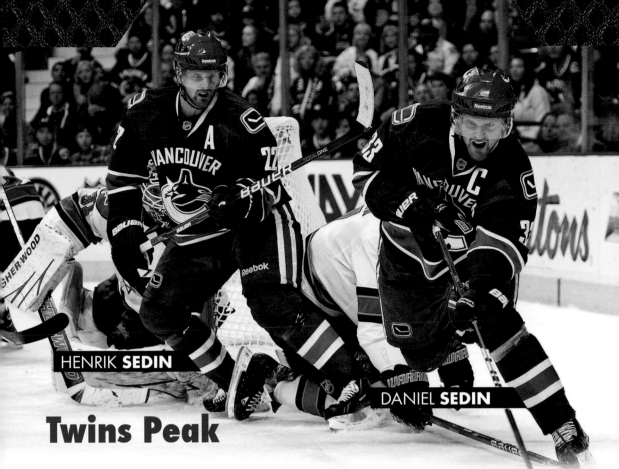

HENRIK **SEDIN**

DANIEL **SEDIN**

Twins Peak

In 1999 the Vancouver Canucks made a savvy move to secure the second- and third-overall picks in the NHL's summer draft. Their plan? To select identical twin brothers Daniel and Henrik Sedin of Sweden and have them play together. The move paid off as the Sedins became two of the league's top players. Their faces look the same, and so do their games. With Henrik playing center and Daniel playing left wing—usually on the same line—they have combined for more than 500 goals and 1,600 points in their first 13 seasons.

STAT-TASTIC

Jonathan Quick allowed just six goals in six games in the 2012 Stanley Cup Finals to lead the Los Angeles Kings to their first championship.

Doing It All

Hockey players have different roles for their teams. Not every forward is a goal scorer or a set-up man. Some are defensive specialists, assigned to check opposing players and keep pucks out of harm's way. The NHL awards the Selke Trophy to the best defensive forward of the year. Recent winners have included:

- Patrice **Bergeron**, Boston Bruins, 2014, 2012
- Jonathan **Toews**, Chicago Blackhawks, 2013
- Ryan **Kesler**, Vancouver Canucks, 2011
- Pavel **Datsyuk**, Detroit Red Wings, 2010, 2009, 2008
- Rod **Brind'Amour**, Carolina Hurricanes, 2007, 2006

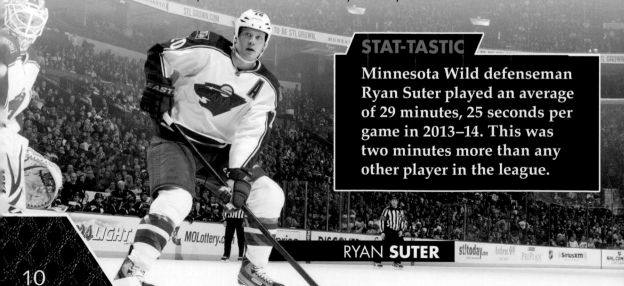

STAT-TASTIC

Minnesota Wild defenseman Ryan Suter played an average of 29 minutes, 25 seconds per game in 2013–14. This was two minutes more than any other player in the league.

RYAN **SUTER**

The Magic Man

Is he a wizard or a thief? That's a question opponents often ask about Pavel Datsyuk. The Detroit Red Wings star center is considered one of the best two-way forwards in the game, meaning he excels at both ends of the rink. On defense he uses his stick like a magic wand, making pucks disappear from foes' blades. Before opponents realize what has happened, "Magic Man" has turned steals into goals at the other end of the arena.

PAVEL **DATSYUK**

REMARKABLE RECORDS

At 6-foot-9 (2.00 meters), Boston Bruins defenseman Zdeno Chara is the tallest player to skate in the NHL. When wearing skates, he's nearly 7 feet (2.13 m) tall!

Shootout in Sochi

On February 15, 2014, T.J. Oshie coasted down the center of the rink for the sixth time. He waited for an opening and then snapped a wrist shot between the goalie's legs. The shootout goal won the game for Team USA against the home team in the 2014 Winter Olympics in Sochi, Russia. Oshie scored on four of six shootout tries that day to break a tie game. It's why he was there. He is one of the best shootout specialists in the NHL, with a 56 percent success rate over his career with the St. Louis Blues.

STAT-TASTIC

In 2011–12 Ilya Kovalchuk of the New Jersey Devils set a record for most shootout goals in a season by netting an incredible 11 goals.

T.J. **OSHIE**

Tiger Williams racked up 3,966 penalty minutes over 14 seasons, a record. In 1974–75, the Philadelphia Flyers' Dave Schultz was penalized 472 minutes, a single-season record.

DAVE **SCHULTZ**

Icy Enforcers

While there are some fans who don't believe fighting should be allowed in hockey, it does happen from time to time. Several teams employ enforcers—tough guys whose job it is to protect their team's best players. Those fighters often end up with a load of penalty minutes. On March 31, 1991, the Bruins' Chris "Knuckles" Nilan was penalized a record 10 times in the same game. He spent a whopping 42 minutes in the penalty box.

Who You Callin' Old?

Jaromir Jagr says that he wants to play hockey until he's 50. That might not be as far-fetched as it sounds. After finishing the season 2014–15 season with the Florida Panthers, Jagr was the league's all-time leader in game-winning goals and fourth all-time in scoring. At the age of 43, the nine-time All-Star signed a new one-year contract with the Panthers in April of 2015.

JAROMIR **JAGR**

REMARKABLE RECORDS

The oldest player to skate in the NHL was the great Gordie Howe. He retired at age 52 after 32 professional seasons and 2,186 games.*

Seasons and games include NHL and WHA career

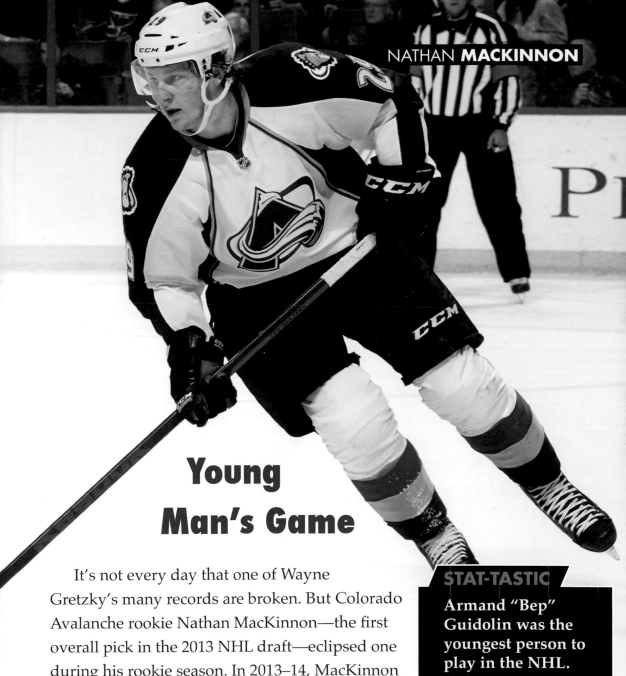

Young Man's Game

It's not every day that one of Wayne Gretzky's many records are broken. But Colorado Avalanche rookie Nathan MacKinnon—the first overall pick in the 2013 NHL draft—eclipsed one during his rookie season. In 2013–14, MacKinnon scored at least one point in 13 consecutive games. That is now the longest streak by a player age 18 or younger. The 18-year-old Gretzky had a point in 12 straight games.

STAT-TASTIC

Armand "Bep" Guidolin was the youngest person to play in the NHL. He was 16 years, 11 months old when he first suited up for the Boston Bruins in 1942.

Goofball Goalie

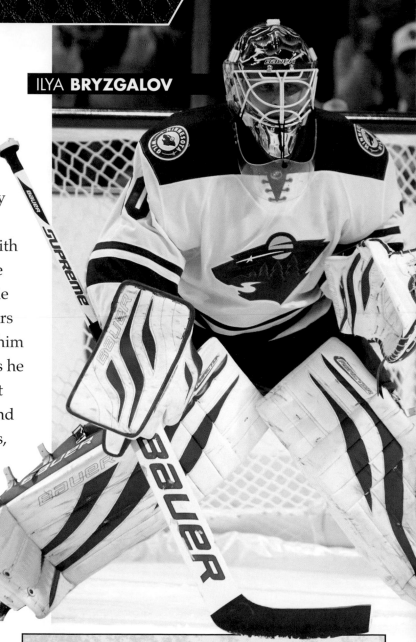

ILYA **BRYZGALOV**

Goaltender Ilya Bryzgalov may have the quirkiest personality in the NHL. He's been known to take selfies with fans while sitting on the bench as a backup goalie during a game. Reporters can't wait to interview him to hear the funny things he says. When asked about facing Sidney Crosby and the Pittsburgh Penguins, Bryz famously said, "You know, I'm not afraid of anything. I'm afraid of bears—bears in the forest."

REMARKABLE RECORDS

In 2012–13, Chicago Blackhawks goaltender Ray Emery became the first goaltender in NHL history to start a season with 12 consecutive wins.

Dog Lover

St. Louis Blues forward David Backes is a dog lover. But he doesn't just enjoy having them as pets. He and his wife fly around the United States to rescue homeless and neglected dogs and help them find good homes. After playing for Team USA in the 2014 Olympics, Backes returned to St. Louis with two stray dogs that were hanging around the Olympic Village in Sochi, Russia. The dogs went to good homes in the United States.

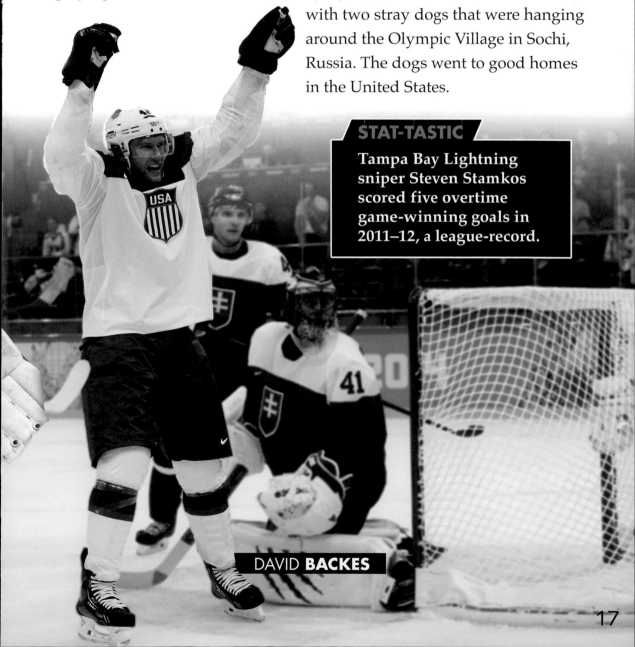

STAT-TASTIC

Tampa Bay Lightning sniper Steven Stamkos scored five overtime game-winning goals in 2011–12, a league-record.

DAVID **BACKES**

Chapter 2

AGED GREATS

WAYNE **GRETZKY**

Most Hart Trophies	
Wayne **Gretzky**	9
Gordie **Howe**	6
Eddie **Shore**	4
Bobby **Clarke**	3
Mario **Lemieux**	3
Howie **Morenz**	3
Bobby **Orr**	3
Alex **Ovechkin**	3

Most Norris Trophies (top defenseman)	
Bobby **Orr**	8
Doug **Harvey**	7
Nicklas **Lidstrom**	7
Raymond **Bourque**	5
Chris **Chelios**	3
Paul **Coffey**	3
Pierre **Pilote**	3
Denis **Potvin**	3

STAT-TASTIC

Take away Wayne Gretzky's goal total, and he would have enough assists to still be the NHL's all-time leading scorer.

The Great One(s)

Who is the greatest hockey player of all time? A case can be made for Gordie Howe, who scored crafty goals and dished out assists as sharp as his elbows. Bobby Orr forever changed the way defensemen played the game in the offensive zone. But Wayne Gretzky came along, shattered records, and then put those marks way out of reach. He's the all-time leader in points (2,857), goals (894), assists (1,963), and hat tricks (50). He's the only player to score 200 points in a single season, and he did that four times. No wonder the entire NHL retired his jersey number—99.

REMARKABLE RECORDS

Bobby Orr is the only defenseman to lead the NHL in scoring, and he did it twice with 120 points in 1969–70 and 135 in 1974–75. His all-time best season was 1970–71 when he scored 139 points, including 102 assists.

BOBBY **ORR**

MARIO **LEMIEUX**

Five for Five

They called him Super Mario, and he was a super scorer. The Pittsburgh Penguins' Mario Lemieux led the NHL in scoring six times. Only Wayne Gretzky did it more. But on New Year's Eve, 1988, Lemieux did something that neither Gretzky nor anyone else in the league has ever done. He scored five goals in five different situations: even strength, power play, short-handed, penalty-shot, and empty-net.

STAT-TASTIC

Dave Andreychuk, who played for six different teams between 1982 and 2006, scored more power-play goals than anyone in NHL history with 274.

Goalie Scores a Goal

Fourteen goals in NHL history have been credited to goaltenders, including three by New Jersey Devils great Martin Brodeur. In some cases, the goalie gets credit as the last player from the scoring team to touch the puck. In seven others, including one of Brodeur's goals, the goaltender fired the puck the length of the ice, nearly 200 feet (60 m) and into the net. Here are those goals:

- Ron **Hextall**, Philadelphia Flyers, 1987

- Ron **Hextall**, Philadelphia Flyers, 1989

- Chris **Osgood**, Detroit Red Wings, 1996

- Martin **Brodeur**, New Jersey Devils, 2000

- Jose **Theodore**, Montreal Canadiens, 2001

- Evgeni **Nabokov**, San Jose Sharks, 2002

- Mike **Smith**, Phoenix Coyotes, 2013

REMARKABLE RECORDS

In 2009 Martin Brodeur broke Terry Sawchuk's legendary record of 103 career shutouts. Brodeur now has the most games played (1,266), wins (691), and shutouts (125) in NHL history.

MARTIN **BRODEUR**

21

Goals Through the Years

Scoring goals has always been important. Here are the top goal scorers in each full decade of pro hockey history.

Decade:	Player:	Goals:
1920s	Babe **Dye**	190
1930s	Charlie **Conacher**	198
1940s	Maurice **Richard**	250
1950s	Gordie **Howe**	376
1960s	Bobby **Hull**	440
1970s	Phil **Esposito**	509
1980s	Wayne **Gretzky**	626
1990s	Brett **Hull**	464
2000s	Jarome **Iginla**	350

STAT-TASTIC

Joe Malone holds the record for most goals scored in a game with seven. Malone's record has stood since 1920.

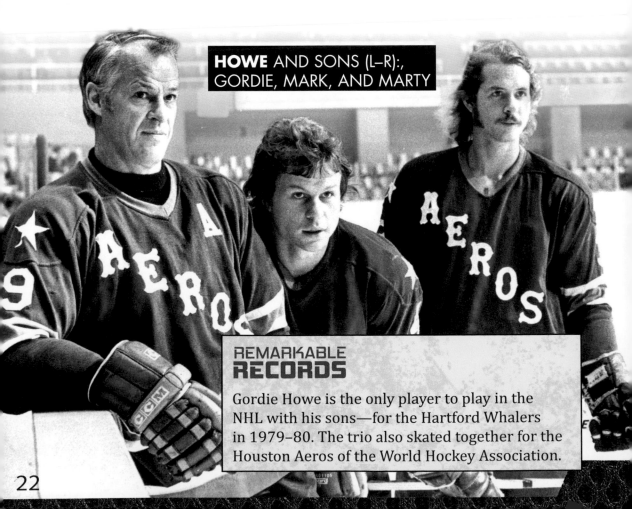

HOWE AND SONS (L–R):, GORDIE, MARK, AND MARTY

REMARKABLE RECORDS

Gordie Howe is the only player to play in the NHL with his sons—for the Hartford Whalers in 1979–80. The trio also skated together for the Houston Aeros of the World Hockey Association.

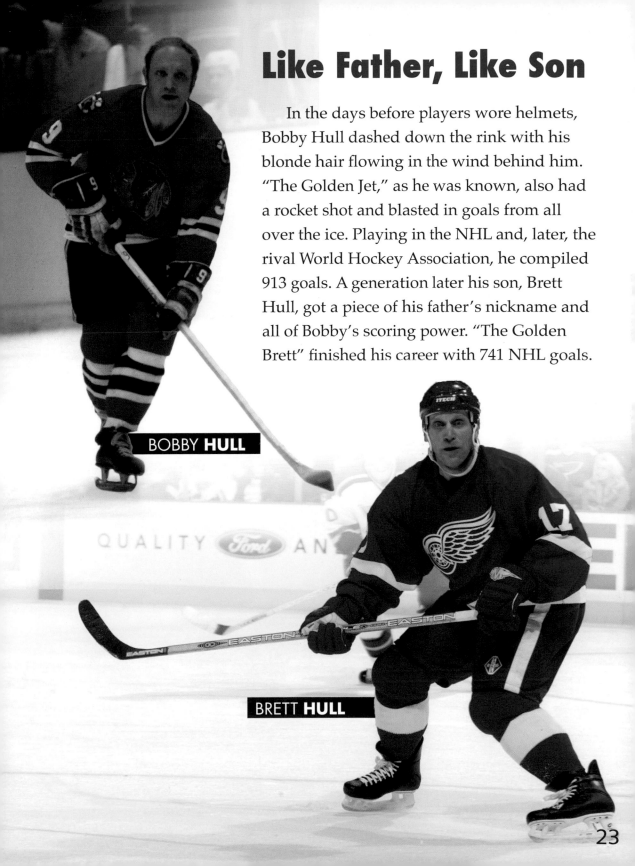

Like Father, Like Son

In the days before players wore helmets, Bobby Hull dashed down the rink with his blonde hair flowing in the wind behind him. "The Golden Jet," as he was known, also had a rocket shot and blasted in goals from all over the ice. Playing in the NHL and, later, the rival World Hockey Association, he compiled 913 goals. A generation later his son, Brett Hull, got a piece of his father's nickname and all of Bobby's scoring power. "The Golden Brett" finished his career with 741 NHL goals.

BOBBY **HULL**

BRETT **HULL**

Chapter 3

TERRIFIC TEAMS

Championship Format

The NHL recognizes nine dynasties throughout its history. These teams became the dominant forces for a span of several years.

Team:	Years:	Titles:
Ottawa **Senators**	1919–27	4
Toronto **Maple Leafs**	1946–51	4
Detroit **Red Wings**	1949–55	4
Montreal **Canadiens**	1956–60	5
Toronto **Maple Leafs**	1961–67	4
Montreal **Canadiens**	1964–69	4
Montreal **Canadiens**	1970–75	4
New York **Islanders**	1979–83	4
Edmonton **Oilers**	1983–90	5

NEW YORK **ISLANDERS**, 1963 NHL STANLEY CUP CHAMPS

REMARKABLE RECORDS

The Montreal Canadiens are the NHL's most successful franchise. They have won a record 24 Stanley Cup championships, including one before the league even existed.

Clearly Canadiens

How good were the Montreal Canadiens of the 1950s and '60s? So good that the NHL needed to change the rules to help out opposing teams. Snipers such as Rocket Richard, Boom-Boom Geoffrion, and Jean Beliveau were too good on the power play. They often scored more than one goal during a two-minute minor penalty. So the league decided to allow the penalized player out of the box once a goal was scored.

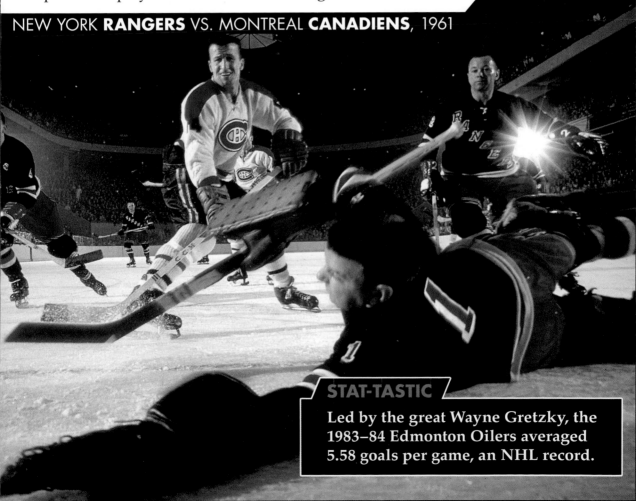

NEW YORK **RANGERS** VS. MONTREAL **CANADIENS**, 1961

STAT-TASTIC

Led by the great Wayne Gretzky, the 1983–84 Edmonton Oilers averaged 5.58 goals per game, an NHL record.

No Love Lost

The Boston Bruins and the Montreal Canadiens don't like each other very much. The teams first started playing each other in 1924 and have met more than 900 times, including the postseason. The rivalry heats up in the playoffs, where the teams have squared off a record 34 times, including in seven Stanley Cup Finals. Montreal usually has had the upper hand in the postseason. The Canadiens are 25–9 in those playoff series, including a 7–0 mark in the Finals.

REMARKABLE RECORDS

The Chicago Blackhawks and the Detroit Red Wings have played the most regular-season games against each other. Going into the 2014–15 season, they met 727 times.

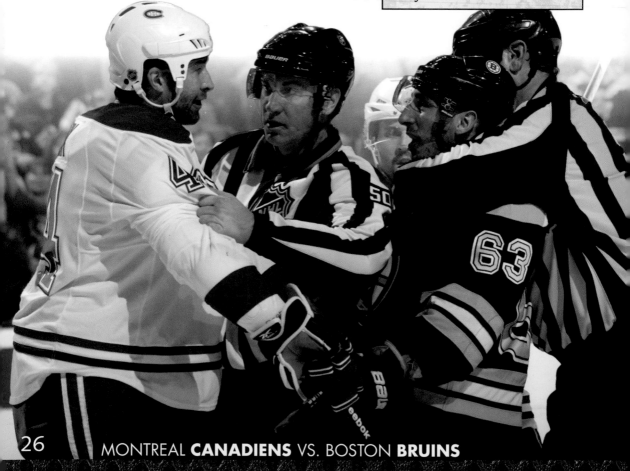

Battle for Pennsylvania

When the NHL doubled the size of the league, adding six new franchises in 1967, it put teams at both ends of Pennsylvania. The Pittsburgh Penguins and the Philadelphia Flyers quickly became archrivals. The teams have had some epic regular- and postseason battles. One included an eight-point game (five goals, three assists) by Penguins great Mario Lemieux in the 1989 playoffs. The teams also played a five-overtime thriller in 2000 that ended when the Flyers' Keith Primeau fired in the game-winning goal.

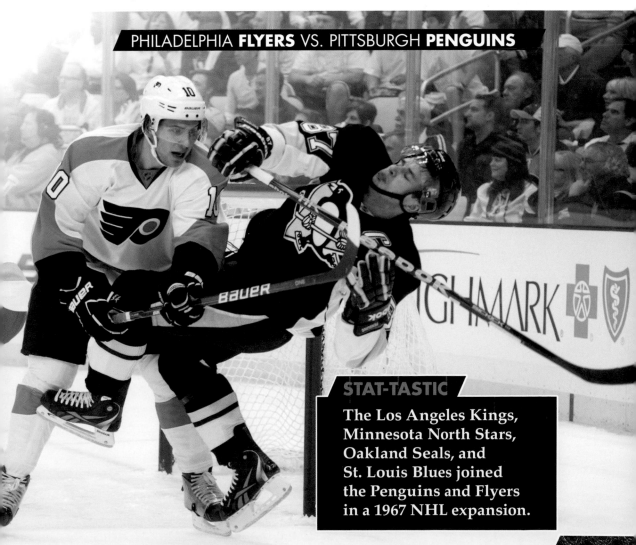

PHILADELPHIA **FLYERS** VS. PITTSBURGH **PENGUINS**

STAT-TASTIC

The Los Angeles Kings, Minnesota North Stars, Oakland Seals, and St. Louis Blues joined the Penguins and Flyers in a 1967 NHL expansion.

The Original Six

From 1942 until 1967, The Original Six were the only teams in the league. Before that era, several other franchises came and went. Some even won Stanley Cup championships. However, those teams didn't have the lasting power of the originals.

Original Six		
Boston **Bruins**	Detroit **Red Wings**	New York **Rangers**
Chicago **Blackhawks**	Montreal **Canadiens**	Toronto **Maple Leafs**

Other teams that played in the NHL before 1942 include: the Hamilton Tigers, Montreal Maroons, Montreal Wanderers, New York Americans, Philadelphia Quakers, Pittsburgh Pirates, Quebec Bulldogs, St. Louis Eagles, and the original Ottawa Senators, who won three Stanley Cups in the 1920s.

All About the Cup

The Stanley Cup has been awarded as a hockey championship trophy since 1893, more than 20 years before the NHL existed. The Montreal Amateur Athletic Association won it the first two times and four times total. Other early Cup-winning teams included the Ottawa Silver Seven, the Seattle Metropolitans, and the Vancouver Millionaires.

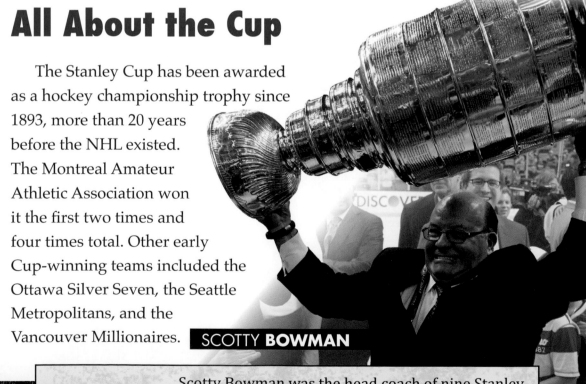

SCOTTY **BOWMAN**

REMARKABLE RECORDS

Scotty Bowman was the head coach of nine Stanley Cups winners. He led the Canadiens to five titles, the Red Wings to three, and the Penguins to one.

WONDERMENTS

Greatest Nicknames

Best Nicknames of Today	
Name	Nickname
Sidney **Crosby**	"Sid the Kid"
Alex **Ovechkin**	"Alexander the Gr8"
Teemu **Selanne**	"The Finnish Flash"
Nikolai **Khabibulin**	"The Bulin Wall"
Jonathan **Toews**	"Captain Serious"
Jarome **Iginla**	"Iggy"
P.K. **Subban**	"The Subbanator"
Paul **Bissonnette**	"BizNasty"
Dustin **Byfuglien**	"Big Buff"
Johan **Franzen**	"Muler"

Best Nicknames of Yesteryear	
Name	Nickname
Wayne **Gretzky**	"The Great One"
Georges **Vezina**	"The Chicoutimi Cucumber"
Bernie **Geoffrion**	"Boom Boom"
Maurice **Richard**	"Rocket"
Henri **Richard**	"Pocket Rocket"
Bobby **Hull**	"The Golden Jet"
Frank **Brimsek**	"Mr. Zero"
Dave **Schultz**	"The Hammer"
Lorne **Worsley**	"Gump"
Gordie **Howe**	"Mr. Hockey"

STAT-TASTIC

Howie Morenz, one of the NHL's first superstars, had several nicknames. They included the Stratford Streak, the Mitchell Meteor, the Canadian Comet, and the Hurtling Habitant.

Greatest Records

Longest game: Red **Wings** 1, Montreal Maroons 0 (6 overtimes; March 24, 1936)

Consecutive point-scoring streak: Wayne **Gretzky**, Oilers, 51 games (1983–84)

Most goals by a rookie: Teemu **Selanne**, Jets, 76 (1992–93)

Fastest hat trick: Bill **Mosienko**, Blackhawks, 21 seconds (March 23, 1952)

Consecutive games played by a goalie: Glenn **Hall**, Red Wings/Blackhawks, 502 (1955–1962)

Most goals by a defenseman in one game: Ian **Turnbull**, Maple Leafs, 5 (1977)

Best career plus-minus: Larry **Robinson**, Canadiens, plus-730

Most shots on goal in a season: Phil **Esposito**, Bruins, 550 (1970–71)

Most wins in the regular season: Detroit **Red Wings**, 62 (1995–96)

Most career points by a goalie: Tom **Barrasso**, 48

Glossary

blue line (BLOO LINE)—a line painted on the ice that marks the end of a team's offensive zone

center (SEN-tur)—the player who participates in a face-off at the beginning of play

defenseman (dih-FENS-muhn)—a player who lines up in a defensive zone to prevent opponents from getting open shots on goal

hat trick (HAT TRIK)—when a player scores three goals in one game

lockout (LOK-out)—a period of time in which owners prevent players from reporting to their teams; owners do not pay players during lockouts and no games are played

plus-minus (PLUS MY-nuhs)—statistic that measures a player's impact on the game; in hockey, a player gains a point when he is on the ice when his team scores and loses a point when he is on the ice and the opponent scores

points (POYNTZ)—a player's total number of goals and assists

power play (POW-ur-PLAY)—when a team has a one- or two-player advantage because the other team has one or more players in the penalty box

rookie (RUK-ee)—a first-year player

Stanley Cup (STAN-lee KUP)—the trophy given each year to the NHL champion

shoot-out (SHOOT-owt)—a method of breaking a tie score at the end of overtime play

wing (WING)—a type of forward who usually stays near the sides of the zone

Read More

Gitlin, Marty. *The Stanley Cup: All About Pro Hockey's Biggest Event.* Winner Takes All. Mankato, Minn.: Capstone, 2013

Frederick, Shane. *Six Degrees of Sidney Crosby: Connecting Hockey Stars.* Six Degrees of Sports. North Mankato, Minn.: Capstone, 2015.

Frederick, Shane. *Ultimate Guide to Pro Hockey Teams 2015.* Sports Illustrated Kids. North Mankato, Minn.: Capstone, 2014.

Internet Sites

FactHound offers a safe, fun way to find Internet sites related to this book. All of the sites on FactHound have been researched by our staff.

Here's all you do:

Visit *www.facthound.com*

Type in this code: 9781476557977

Check out projects, games and lots more at
www.capstonekids.com

Index